These poems, the bittersweet fruit of a malignant place
and time, belie the lightness of their title by inviting
us to remember the immensities behind them - war,
suffering, love and death. Fleeting, disconnected,
they feel like insights jotted on the run between here
and there, Iraq and Ireland, by a man under pressure,
anxious to leave behind him the gleanings of a life.

—Harry Clifton

Brevity is the soul of wit and Majed Mujed's aphoristic
poems, beautifully rendered by the ever-indispensable
Kareem James Abu-Zeid, have a worldly wisdom to
them, and his penchant for surrealist turns and scathing
insights leaves sharp edges here and there, prompting us
to return to them again and again.

—André Naffis-Sahely

Majed Mujed's The Book of Trivialities is a gem of a book;
intimate, tender, thought-provoking and intricately
crafted, these aphoristic fragments contain a wisdom
and humour that marks them as anything but trivial.
These are poems to revisit again and again for their
sharp wit, and their revelatory power.

—Jessica Traynor

The Book of Trivialities

First published in 2023 by Skein Press
skeinpress.com

Design and illustration by Patrick Fisher of Frontwards Design
Arabic typesetting consultancy and typeface by Lara Captan
Typeset in Calluna and Falak OTL
Printed by Henry Ling Limited, at the Dorset Press, Dorchester, UK

A CIP catalogue for this title is available from the British Library.

ISBN 978-1-915017-00-0

Skein Press gratefully acknowledges the financial support it receives
from the Arts Council of Ireland and The Rowan Trust.

The
Book
of
Trivialities

Majed
Mujed

translated by
Kareem James
Abu-Zeid

I.

To love is to have hope.
It's enough to sow a chirping in the earth:
you wait for the sound to sprout
and grow feathers and a beak.

الحبُّ هو أنْ يكون لديك أملٌ
يكفي لتزرع زِقْزِقةً
وتنتظر حتى تنبتَ
ويصير لها ريشٌ ومنقار.

2.

What is the sea?
Raw sky in music's kitchen.
What is music?
A chaos that orchestrates
our vision for life.
What is life?
A question that's running—
when it stops, it dies.
What is the question?
The knower's doubt.
What is doubt?
The heart of certainty.
What is certainty?
Love.
What is love?
We cannot ask that question.

ما البحرُ؟

سماءٌ نيِّئةٌ في مطبخِ الموسيقى،

ما الموسيقى؟

فوضى تنظِّم رؤيتَنا للحياة،

ما الحياة؟

سؤالٌ يركُض ما إنْ يقفُ يموت،

ما السؤال؟

شكُّ العارف،

ما الشكُّ؟

قلبُ اليقين،

ما اليقين؟

أنْ نحبَّ

ما الحبُّ؟

أنْ لا نسأل.

3.

"Have you seen death?"
"No."
"Then you haven't seen life."

= هل رأيتَ الموتَ؟

ـ لا

= إذاً أنتَ لَم ترَ الحياة.

4.

Those who have forgotten their dreams
are smarter than those who,
every moment of their lives,
painfully remember
how they were defeated.

الذين نَسوا أحلامَهم
أكثرُ ذكاءً من أولئك الذين
طوالَ حياتهم يتذكّرون بألمٍ
كـيـــف هزموا.

5.

The wounded foot does not trample,
the wounded hand does not strike,
the wounded eye does not pry,
the wounded heart does not lash out...
It's as if those who are wounded
are more modest, and more noble.

القدمُ الجريحةُ لا تدوس،
اليدُ الجريحةُ لا تضرب،
العينُ الجريحةُ لا تتلصص،
القلبُ الجريحُ لا يجرح،
كأنَّ المجروحين أكثرُ حياءً ونبلاً.

6.

"They're thronging in the boundless void,
so how could they approach your brimming soul?"
asks the man who is alone.

إنّهم يحتشدون في الفراغ الواسع
كيف يأتون إلى روحِكَ الممتلئة؟
يقولُ الوحيد.

7.

The more losses you have,
the more they pile up.
And the more they pile up,
the more dust that's left behind
by your friends as they run from you.

كلّما كثُرتْ خساراتُكَ، كثُرتْ خساراتُك،
وكـلّما كثرتْ خساراتُكَ..
يكثرُ الغبارُ الذي يُخلِّفهُ أصدقاؤك وهم يطيرون.

8.

Let your mind devour books and gulp down sleep,
and in the morning laugh with the dead—
it's life's absurdity that makes them laugh.

دَعْ عقلَكَ يأكلُ القراءةَ ويشربُ النومَ
وفي الصباح اضحكْ مع الموتى،
فالحياةُ من فرطِ سُخفِها صارت تُضحكهم.

9.

Some forgetting is malignant:
it erases all sweetness from the final page
but keeps the bitterness of the opening lines.

بعضُ النسيانِ خبيثٌ
يبدأُ بمحوِ الحُلوِ من الأخير
ويبقي المُرَّ في السطورِ الأولى.

10.

The stench of madness comes from the poet's room.

When they broke down the door
all they found was a rotting book
with regret buzzing around it.

رائحةُ جنونٍ تأتي من غرفةِ الشاعر،
عندما كسروا البابَـ،
لم يجدوا سوى كتابٍ أزرق يطنُّ حولَه الأسف.

II.

Whenever answers fall like rain from the vault of the sky,
the questions ripen, like barley, in the taverns of the earth.

كلّما سقطتْ قطراتُ إجاباتٍ من قُبةِ السماءِ،
نَضُجتِ الأسئلةُ مثلَ الشعيرِ في حاناتِ الأرض.

12.

"I found an axe head in the woods," a tree said.
And another replied:
"This slab of steel will do nothing
as long as we don't give it
any of our wood."

وجَدْتُ رأسَ فأسٍ في الغابة، قالت شجرة.
قالت شجرةٌ أخرى:
لَنْ تفعل شيئاً قطعةُ الحديدِ هذه
إنْ لَم تدخل فيها خَشبةٌ مِنّا.

13.

The rose: "How I wish I could be like you."
The apple: "Why?"
The rose: "Because then I'd be a rose,
            and an apple, too."

الوردةُ: كَمْ أتمنّى أنْ أكونَ مثلكِ.

التفاحة: لِماذا؟

الوردةُ: لأنّي حينها سأكونُ وردةً وتفاحة.

14.

The woman who reveals her body
to a man who's neither poet nor musician
doesn't know
her body's nothing more than a dictionary
or an instrument.

الأنثى التي تكشفُ جسدَها لغير شاعرٍ أو عازف،
هي لا تعرفُ أنَّ جسدَها
ليس أكثرَ من معجمٍ لغويّ
أو آلةً موسيقية.

15.

"Speak into my other ear, please."
"Are you hard of hearing?"
"No, it's just that one of my ears
is for listening to music."

= أَدُرْ فَمَكَ إلى أذني الثانية.

ـ هل سمعُ أذنك هذه ثقيل؟

= لا.. لكنها فقط لسماع الموسيقى.

16.

Life, sometimes, is a gentle song.
It escapes from all the idle talk
into the street,
but a quick scream runs it over.

الحياةُ –أحياناً– أغنيةٌ ناعمةٌ،
تهربُ من ضجيج اللغو إلى الشارع،
فيدهسها صراخٌ سريع.

17.

Sometimes, from on high, the mind of a hungry bird
sees every wave as a piece of meat—
although the fish is far off,
deep in the heart of the sea.

أحياناً، يرى عقلُ الطائر الجائع من الأعلى،
كلَّ موجةٍ قطعةَ لحم،
بينما الأسماكُ بعيدةٌ في قلبِ البحر العميق.

18.

Sometimes a man wants
to place all the words in a coffin
and weep bitter tears
because he's spoken them before.

أحياناً يتمنى الإنسان
أنْ يضعَ كلَّ الكلام في تابوت
ويبكي عنده بكاءً حارّا
لأنه قالهُ ذاتَ يوم.

19.

Sometimes *I love you* becomes a sea,
and when I say it, I become a boat
and the air I breathe
is as wind in the sail of dreams.

أحياناً تصيرُ كلمةُ (أحبكِ) بحراً،
وأصيرُ أنا حين أقولُها زورقاً،
والهواءُ الذي أتنفّسُهُ
يدفعُ شراعَ الأحلامِ نحوكِ.

20.

The bed's not big enough for the three of us.
Please now,
    tell modesty to sleep somewhere else.

السريرُ لا يكفينا، نحن الثلاثة،
لذا أرجوكِ دعي الحياةَ ينامُ في مكانٍ آخر.

21.

The sick breast the doctor cut off
and buried in the hospital garden—
on the second day, a river of blue cries,
full of children, flowed out from it.

النهدُ المريضُ الذي قطعه الطبيبُ
ودفنَهُ في حديقةِ المستشفى
تدفّق منه في اليومِ الثاني
نهرٌ من الصُّراخ الأزرق مليءٌ بالأطفال.

22.

The man who weeps
remains just a man, but his eyes
become two women.

الرجلُ الذيــ يبكي
يصيرُ رجلاً وامرأتين.

23.

Wherever she looks, two roses and a butterfly sprout.
And when the breeze puts its mouth on her neck
while she's sleeping, flowers bloom
and butterflies burst from her fingers.

أينما تَنظرُ تنبتُ وردتان وفَراشةٌ
وحين يضعُ الهواءُ فمَهُ على رقبتها وهي نائمة
تتفتح الزهرتان
وتفورُ من أصابِعِها الفراشات.

24.

The Story:
A little light suddenly fell upon a stranger on the street of the night,
he looked up to see where it came from:
A woman caught in insomnolence was staring at him
and when he lowered his head and walked on,
she let out some kind of curse, and closed the window.

*

The Poem:
Lowering his head, a stranger asked himself, What is hope?
And his self replied: A woman who tosses a rose of light, waits,
and when she's ignored curses her luck and closes her eyes,
while the scent of her body fills the darkness.

الحكاية

..

كان ثمّةَ ضوءٌ قليلٌ سقط فجأةً أمامَ غريبٍ في شارع الليل،
نظرَ إلى الأعلى قليلاً ليعرف من أين أتى،
كانت سيدةٌ عالقةٌ في الأرقِ تنظرُ إليه،
حين أحنى رأسَهُ ومشى،
شَتمَتْ شيئاً ما، وأغلقتْ نافذتَها.

*

القصيدة

..

قال غريبٌ لنفسِهِ وهو محنيُّ الرأس: ما هو الأمل؟
قالتْ نفسُهُ: سيدةٌ ترمي وردةَ ضوءٍ وتنتظر،
حين تُهملُ، تَشتمُ حظَّها، تُغلقُ عينيها
وتُدخِلُ شذىً جسدِها في الظلام.

25.

A poet who's a peasant
and a poet who's a housewife:
He goes out and brings her grains of salt and red pepper
while she gratefully readies the pot.
In this way, each day the world's disturbed between them.
In this way, each day they dance,
he a spoon bearing salt and pepper,
she a pot wherein a white hope ripples,
they spin, and like this, they write a child.
As soon as the dots flow out to crown the letters,
they sit, surprised, and wait,
until words grow, and become poetry.

شاعرٌ فلّاحٌ وشاعرةٌ ربّةُ بيت،
هو يذهبُ ويأتيها بترابِ الملح والفلفل الأحمر،
وهي ممتنّةٌ تهيئ له الماعون الأبيض،
هكذا كلَّ يومٍ يضطربُ العالمُ بينهما،
هكذا كلَّ يوم يدوران،
هو ملعقةٌ تضعُ ترابَ الملح والفلفل الأحمر
وهي ماعونٌ يتموّج فيه رجاءٌ أبيض،
يدوران لكي يكتبان طفلاً،
وما إنْ تتدفَّقُ النقاطُ وتصيرَ على الحروف
يجلسان مندهشين وينتظران،
حتى تكبرَ القصيدةُ ويصيرَ فيها شعرٌ.

About Solstice Stories

The Book of Trivialities is part of the *Solstice Stories* series from Skein Press, featuring creative collaborations between contemporary writers, translators and artists. Launched in 2022, *Solstice Stories* is designed to be a celebration of the small, the brilliant, and the beautiful, seeking to stimulate conversations and inspire hope by reconnecting us with our imaginations and bringing people and communities together.

About the translator

Kareem James Abu-Zeid, PhD, is a freelance translator of poets and novelists from across the Arab world who translates from Arabic, French, and German. His work has won numerous awards and accolades, including the 2022 Sarah Maguire Prize for Poetry in Translation for the Palestinian poet Najwan Darwish's book *Exhausted on the Cross* (NYRB Poets, 2021). He is also the author of *The Poetics of Adonis and Yves Bonnefoy: Poetry as Spiritual Practice* (Lockwood, 2019). His most recent translation is *Chaos, Crossing* by Olivia Elias (World Poetry Books, 2022).

About the author

Majed Mujed was born in Iraq in 1971 and has lived in Ireland since 2015. One of the founders of the Iraqi House of Poetry, he worked as a journalist and publisher in the Iraqi cultural press for twenty years. He has published five collections of poetry in Arabic and has garnered awards for his work from the Al Mada Cultural Foundation, Iraqi House of Wisdom and Iraqi Intellectuals Conference. He is the recipient of a Play It Forward Fellowship (2021) and Agility Award (2022) from the Arts Council of Ireland.